CRUDE

POEMS

Taylor Brorby

Ice Cube Press, LLC
North Liberty, Iowa, USA

For Logan, Noah, Alexander, and Oliver

The pen is mightier than the pump jack.

How we treat our land, how we build upon it, how we act toward our air and water, in the long run, will tell what kind of people we really are.
—Laurance S. Rockefeller

Always do what you are afraid to do.
—Ralph Waldo Emerson

MANIFESTO

Thrum in the cracks of soggy river logs
nestled next to the fungus and bacteria
about to bloom into mighty mushrooms.
Squeeze of sage between fingers, its oil
a musk of wildness. Calling out to the
cottonwoods and herons and beavers
I slip into the icy Knife River in spring
then lie down on brambly prairie dirt
cotton white clouds sailing across the sky.

I.

THE AGES HAVE BEEN AT WORK

Those silent sentinels
grass and butte, stream and rock
chambers of the global heart
worked by the ages
grow in might
on the hissing prairies.
On the hard bedrock
I wait for a revelation of meadowlark,
bison, cougar, and coyote.

Trickster, what is it you know?
What ripples across
the waves of a deep lake of being?
Tell me the secrets
of those matters of blood
too deep for words.

As I scrape the edges of canyon walls—
mica, granite, and sandstone—I hear
the crumbling high-speed life.

I climb buttes and bluffs
searching for holy ground
the night sky on fire.

The small break of dirt
as grass climbs higher, what heights
does the prairie measure as thunderheads
billow like a shook blanket against the wind.

LITTLE MISSOURI

To wake up to the purple pink sunrise siltstone slide
into seams, a needle weaving through fabric.

Kingfishers duck and dive, seek silver fish, glittering
coins in your crevices.

Slide over rocks that cause your skin to ripple and roil,
deer flick delicate tongues, steal your blood to fuel
their bodies.

Bison lumber and heave their burly bodies, your space
transgressed by every winged and wooly thing.

As the sun sizzles its dying rays upon your breast, what
sends fright through your veins as saltwater spills from
pump jacks?

EARTHEN VESSELS

In the stubble behind my house
fish too small for words from the
muddy creek. The brown green
hills spread like Moses parting the
sea. I became a pirate then an
artist then a sailor. The infinite
rests in finitude. Mice snatched
by hawks in the golden field
coyotes trotted for a meager
meal. I knew danger lurked in
this still place amidst
the serenity of wild things.

PALLID STURGEON

The armored tank of the prairie, a
letter from the dinosaurs. Sliding in
silt, you sift to the riverbed, hunker
down, slurp roots and minnows
through your vacuum mouth. Five
rows of plates plank your body, a
70-million-year seal of safety—until
now, oil swirling in the eddies of
rivers, gateway to extinction.

Your black eyes gazing into
tomorrow, you warm with the
whiteness of old age, a century of
certainty behind you—swim
through the maelstrom, to the end
of compassion, your certain
demise.

THE HUNT

Five pump jacks circle the state park,
a ring of fire flashing in the distance
as I hike. To hunt bison, the Arikara
burned dry prairie grass, fireworks
erupted over hills, spread
like rippled waves across the sea
of grass. Fire drove bison over
cliffs, into corners, circled them.
Bison died on impact, skulls cracked,
crimson blood poured over brown fur,
their black tongues dried from the heat.
I walk in this circle of flares and my
nostrils burn, eyes water as fire closes in.

JUNEBERRIES

My small hands, next to grandmother's liver-spotted
hands, roll ripe balls between little fingers like
squinting to look into a crystal ball. For every two
berries dropped in the bucket one finds its way to
my wine-colored tongue. My teeth clamp down, a
flood of nectar—sweet with heat of long days.

My Bridgeman's ice cream pail stained with the
blood of juneberries. A family of pickers finds
glinting berries heavy with the summer sweat of rain.

This place, hidden among brambles in the Missouri
River Valley—silver hair flashes through the green
foliage like a lighthouse onshore.

SWEETNESS

Sage like sweet cigar smoke
fills my lungs with prairie.
This is why we walk: to push aside
clay and clover, to dust our pant
legs with green gray pollen, sage oil
oozing into pores. To crush it
between thumb and finger press it
into journals fill pages with the
wide open space of prairie—
windswept, omnipresent as salt in
the ocean. I want to hoard it like
emeralds, keep its secret hidden
deep within this land, worrying that
its whispering will draw others
here, that ancient call that brings
the traveler home, back to the
sweet smell of sage which is to say
back to ourselves.

SQUARE BUTTE CREEK

Girdles chocolate colored mud
as it flows towards the Mighty Mo
where Lewis and Clark dug hickory
oars into the current, wondered
what the current carried, beyond
the crook of the river.

Here water springs from the coarse
soil of Oliver County, from rich cropland
laden with wheat, oats, barley,
and beets, those crimson
colored vessels of the land.

Where sight vanishes and memory
begins, slips below the surface,
pike float, suspended by hunger,
ready to hurl towards meat, towards
desire, craving the fuel of flesh.

Serenaded by switchgrass, I slip
into the symphony of sound.

COTEAU

Glacier of my childhood,
I loved you though I didn't know.
The potholes—pools of calved ice—
mirrors across the prairie, rippling
hills, mounds of bread
crumbs the ice dolloped on the
trail towards home, rocks
and pebbles, letters left from the great
white north, no return necessary.

My playground, the glacier's footprint
slicing Dakota in half like an apple—
not quick, not like ripping
a band aid. More like the slow
letter press, imprinting
symbols on paper, inking
the shifting page of the world.

Before I was born, before
the Revolution, the Magna
Carta; before Christ, Socrates, or
Cleopatra, the glacier left traces
in sand; before Mosaic Law
and pyramids. Before we knew ice
carved and pressed canyons into
homes of wonder, shaped rivers
into arteries of continent,
layering chocolate soil.

My love gurgles like a stream,
snaps like strong wheat, slinks
like sand, for glaciers as they
slip behind the curtain, exit
the stage, forever.

OIL
—after John Donne

You ooze and flow over every rock
and crevice, looking for an outlet
into the free market of my soul
whose price you have taken captive
whose beauty you hold ransom.
Why can't we leave you under rock
where pressure and force can hold
you at bay? Toxic, your force is too
much—you slather your hands and
dap your knuckles as you count with
fisted fury the almighty dollar singing
God Bless America. But I will not
call you blessed. Destroyer of land,
you shall not enter here, the sweet
space of my longing. Stay in place.
Four hundred million years of work
shaped and formed you and another
four hundred million years will
bring you to mighty ruin.

LITTLE MISSOURI STATE PARK

North on Highway 22
driving out of Dickinson
dipping into a land
of Indian wars, past
Killdeer Mountain,
where General Sully,
sent by Lincoln,
slit throats as arrows
fell on dry ground.
Further north, new statues
of liberty flare gas
and burn through
the night, past ridges
run with oil rigs.
I slip into a sanctuary
of chirping grasshoppers,
silver sage, stippled clay
decide to hike the new normal,
a pump jack in the distance.

PRETTY BUTTE

I don't want to climb you.
You look like a bitch—
steep and intimidating,
like a woman who paints

her lips red just to titillate
the boys in the bar. You lured
me in with thorny charm.
So I climb, rip at your skin.

Like a lover, I pull at sage
and sweet clover, a beau
ripping your head back
in delight. I follow scoria

curves painted red
by electric fire smoldering
deep in your veins.
I wanted your name

to be a misnomer,
wrapped in swells
of sweet clover,
you looked regal

from a distance.
At the summit I study
your curves up close,
sit in your cool shade.

Smitten by your firmness,
I forget why I came.

WHITE EARTH VALLEY

In the crook of my mind you sit sideways
like a saddle hitched to a horse. You shake
the hills to the horizon like a piece of foil
glinting in the sun. Ash, elms, and birch
dance as their roots sink deep into your
skin, hug against the soft beat of the
river flowing through your valley. When
they came with their steel and grit and
flame, did you quiver like a flower in the
wind, did you open your arms, fling open the
gate, display yourself against a commotion
of sound and say, Take me as I am? No,
not you, you gentle valley. The sun
continued to shine as they came, as they
ripped and dug and dipped into your
pores, taking what they could—like
hungry children stealing cookies from a
cracked jar. As I float down the river I
long to know what you know. Tell me,
what was it like to have glaciers push
against you, moving rock against sand
against ice against time. Does your surface
crack like dry skin, break when pulled too
taut—or does the rain that ripples down
your sides, running rivulets of wonder
bring you rest. Sage of the ages, where
does your strength come from?

HANDEL'S HORIZON

I sit on a butte, peer down a rabbit
hole look west, like Lewis and
Clark, search for the rumored
passageway. Clouds furl like smoke
from a put-out fire. The flicker of
flame dying against the night.
Cobalt cajoles among purples,
lavenders, turquoise. The sun
streaks and breaks the clouds.
Billows pulse and swell.

Handel, slamming
open his shutters shouted,
What are the billows?

A stumbling man, blear-eyed
looked up at the potbellied
German, *The waves!*

Handel muttered over his candle-lit
score, closed his raven-clawed eyes
The waves!

Waves meet me on the horizon,
whisper like the sun-scorched
scoria, saying, All manner of thing
shall be well.

HILLS

Behind the wheat fields over hills
my frail bones bore the weight of
tackle, rod, and reel, paint, canvas,
and palette. I fingered through
reeds, past lonesome cottonwood
trees, guarded against the burning
noonday sun. In a channel stream
kept secret from friends and family,
I sat, slept in wonder, and captured
the color of nature. Along muddied
banks I threw lures hurled like rocks
to hook the furious pike.

FLIGHT

pull your jackknife, release the reel like
a trout into the stream, take hold of
the cord like a chicken about to flop in
headless flight, cut the twine bound
to your heart, release dreams
too small for this world, and know
tomorrow is another wild-full day.

PRAIRIE

silent as a whisper
where wind fingers through
wheat and ripples over rough
bark of cottonwoods. Do not drill,
rip, scrape where water ebbs along
muddy river banks where
prairie wheat tosses the sun
like a copper coin. The buttes
awash in pink, orange, purple, blue,
cranberry. Prairie, like my grandmother's
wedding band handed down through
bloodlines of land, water, sky, air—
our very arteries pillaged,
lungs, skin, and sweat grown toxic
drilled, ripped, scraped,
brought to ruin.

BIGHORN

Custer's fractured skull leaches
cranberry blood, colors his golden
locks red against the brown-stippled
prairie. Buffalo Calf Road Woman
pants, lungs heave. She drops her
club, streaked crimson and walks
towards the general. Custer wheezes.
Glazed eyes against a creek of
blood, life seeps down the coulee.
She clasps Custer's face and turns it
against the sun—lets out her victory
cry, the beginning of silence,
beginning of pain.

CLIMBING BUTTES

Press my feet into bentonite
scrape my sandals against scoria
as I pull sage from the side
of the tombstones of the Rockies.
I carry bourbon in my backpack
fill a flask with muddied river water
add a single droplet to my drink
a bourbon and branch my trophy
when I ascend prairie mountains.
I drive dusty rock roads sweep
through carpeted clover dive
into the bad lands of my
childhood imagination. Rusted
weather vanes swing in the breeze
mark the grave of a never known
farmstead. I dance the sage brush
step at the top of the butte and notice
pump jacks flare in the distance.

EULOGY
—for the Badlands

You were beautiful
a rough land of rock
awash in fuchsia, cobalt,
sienna. Your spinal cord
of scoria granite and quartz
sturdy glistened in the noonday
sun. Arteries of streams
muddied and brown
pumped through your core,
life in a quiet way. But the world
destroys beautiful things.

What is it like to look over
the horizon and see
nothing but ruin? Your
permanence lost in the veil
of progress, a veneer of fortune.
On your deathbed you whispered
to me as flares flickered in your
eyes of delight. Tears muddied
my face and you said, Risk hope.

II.

PUMP JACK

You plant your feet firm into soil
cock your head back in wild delight
as you plunge and pull crude
from deep within earth's sacred core.

You look right then left, peck hard
like a chicken against scratch
hoping no eyes take out their
telescopes glint in an excited passion.

You work at a fevered pace like a man
against the assembly line, hurry and bury
and pull and pluck and ram into a place
of subtle refuge.

Your heart beats like mosquitos' wings
furious for the last remaining
drop of blood.

CHRISTMAS
—Bakken oil fields

When are you coming home, Daddy?
He told her each week each week he
told her *Next week, Darling, next week*
Daddy is coming home. He said he lied lied
to his daughter each week. Swirled
his bourbon as his eyes searched the
alabaster floor. *She's going to have the best*
Christmas this year. He said she was
getting twenty-five hundred dollars for
Christmas. *That'll make it all worth it*
all worth it all worth it.

QUESTION FOR A BUTTE

When my ear tings
with the whisper of water
coursing through my body—
through your body—
my heart thrums
with the shock
of death, the storied
decay of your body
the flow of water
over stone, cactus
clinging to rock.
What is it like
to be slashed, to have
your throat slit, to bleed
rock from your veins of coal?

CUSTER

Banished to Dakota
after going AWOL
after drinking draughts
of pillaged villages,
after slitting Indian throats.
His blonde curls, bleached
by prairie sun, fumed
his desire to destroy
the established way
of life, the first people
living here, to settle
the frontier for cities
and stagecoaches.
He kept a bobcat
in the cellar, captive
wildness to match
his own desire
for glory, for conquest—
so maniacal, so blinded
that the Arikara
led him straight
into the Battle
of Greasy Grass.

FORT BERTHOLD

In the land of burning ground there is no rest,
only sweat, work, and pain. And courage
is sold for a quick profit from horizon to horizon.
No more green leaves. Pronghorn die faraway
and ruin, the spirit of everything.

THE PLAINS KNOWS BARRACKS
—Fort Buford, 1866

Built of stone and water,
stiff and strong, secured
and fastened to vital prairie
soil at the confluence.
Slashed open the frontier,
slit Indian throats, spread
trade and trappers like a virus
up the Missouri through
the stomach of the country.

COTTONWOOD

Waxy leaves twitch in Missouri River air.
This tree, whose seed, shipped by muddy river
water, knew Lewis and Clark, the scent of sweet
Hidatsa tobacco, the clap of General Sully's
pistol as it shot metal into brown-skinned
bodies. Too, this tree watched the grizzly flee
west, the wolf leave the brown carpet prairie,
and the bobcat clamber in the night. Ring by
ring, this tree inches towards the rippling sky,
sinks roots into the sandy sludge bed of the Big
Muddy. General Custer knew this tree.
Lincoln's four score whispered on the wind,
washed its bark as the frontier split open.

HIS VOICE TRAILED OFF LIKE SMOKE

That man covered
in oil his safety shirt
gold like the noonday
sun had acid holes around
his belly his stomach hair
peeking through like tulips
in spring. Looked down
when he said
he hadn't had a day
off in five months
hadn't seen his nine
year-old daughter in as long
hadn't told her the truth
each week when he talked to
her on the phone.

WORKOUT IN DICKINSON

In the gym men puff up like peacocks
flex and pose their bodies in mirrors
expect to be labeled Hercules, Leonidas,
or Thor. Filled with overtime and cheap
beer, come here for a release, to find out
who's alpha and not omega. *I showed her my*
pump jack last night one of them told his
tattooed buddy. *Pumped her full of my oil*
he said as he picked up his rusted barbell.

BEAR DEN BAY

Shit happens they say happens
every day in the land of fire
in the land of no rest where men
and women drive to the bone
in blear-eyed delight for cash.

Shit spills they say spills often in
the ditches where the knobs are
turned like water flowing to the
hose pouring saltwater into wetlands.

The pipe yelped a fissure of cracks
salted the earth.

The brine coursed its way down
the ravine like an eel flopping
towards the shore.

The leak spilled into the lake
then sucked through a pipe
separated like arteries flowing
into a glass a child raised
towards her mouth.

The sage wilted and shriveled
dried and died on its way back
to the land.

SAGE GROUSE

Warble and whoop
hurl your head in a
display of heat. I sit
behind a lonely sage
bush masked in wildness
soaked deep into clay.
As you throw your chest
skyward through mud
brown wings, I gaze
towards the lek, the circle
of your strut. Your egg yolk
breasts out of sight, like a child
playing Hide and Seek and I
eye your feathered feet with envy.
I crouch lower, my torso caked
in dust and release a silent
prayer for one more spring.

DIVIDE COUNTY

hugs Canada to the north
and lays against Montana's
eastern breast. A landscape
pressed by copper coins
whose basins fill with the
drip drip drip of cold
alkaline water. That land
where dirt and clay enclose
family rips at my chest
breath beating, a train at
the tracks.

SCOTT

They never said what killed him.
Such things are not talked about
in my family. Maybe it's that he
was the baby ten siblings before
him draining away the nourishment
he needed like piglets sucking teats
having their fill. Perhaps it started
when he shot himself in the foot
setting off a bang like a packet of
firecrackers in the night leaving some
wound that festered never healed.
Or was it that his life was marred by
work in oil that oozed into the air
wafted to his nostrils like sweet tobacco
furling and flitting with delight
as it coursed its way into delicate lungs
pink because he didn't smoke
and ripe like an apple for the picking.

When they said it, I sat down.
We don't have a history of it. And yet
it showed up like some bastard child.

I saw him once before he died.
Yelled at Mom for not telling me
that it could be his last weekend.
But it wasn't.

A tumor grew in him
a golf ball one week
baseball the next puffing
and pumping into a basketball.
The sports analogies

kept coming. Did he miss
the shot or did we?

In a cafe in Wenatchee
I got the news. That
four-lettered word fell like
a vase breaking on the floor.

I smoked pot and floated
the river hoped to wash
away my uncle.

I didn't attend his funeral.
His sons told me they
needed me there. I declined—
even at twenty-five
I felt like a child like I needed
to be cradled needed to be told
that it was going to be all right.

WHITE EARTH VALLEY II

Your jaw ripped open
a dentist filling cheek
walls with Novocain
squirting the enamel
of rock and sage
and bluebells with bitter
water. No. Your toes
anesthetized shot
with liquid flame
and numbing saltwater
the pain of ingrown
toenail of rock and grass
about to tear from delicate
skin. No. Your pudenda
touched felt-up by some
intruder without consent,
you lie naked in your stream
bed tears coursing. No.

MANDAREE

In a place few don't know,
past prairie, over bentonite,
across creeks, cancer clusters,

sacred land fumes with flares,
You thought you got
rid of them once

took their land,
relegated them to patches
of brown earth squares

and called them sovereign.
The boom bleeds their blood
now. Flares carry carcinogens
to pink lungs.

LETTER MUCH TOO LATE
—for North Dakota

This won't work anymore. You've
changed too much. I thought
I was ready but you were worn
and weary an impatient teacher.

The cranes no longer stop and slink
through mirror water hunting and
striking at delicate minnows. And when
the pronghorn became rare like a fine
jewel hidden and mysterious their
presence no longer seen only
remembered like a waft of perfume
you straightened like a rod and reminded
me that this was the way of progress.

I tried to change, see the positives turn
the other cheek, then turn the other
cheek too. But when the godwits left you
said you didn't notice even though they
were your favorites.

Are we better off? We the most invasive
species marking our compass on a path
that prides profit.

I pack my bags and place them in a chest
of dreams praying like Julian that
All shall be well all shall be well and all
manner of thing shall be well.

But my monastic recitations rip at my
chest leave me burning with a fever
in a land of fire and a blazing babel of
boys knowing that fuels feed comfort
convenience and complacency.

When I asked about the sage grouse
and the sanctity of throats thrumming
in springtime joy you said that they were
better off elsewhere. So I leave you like a
hiker along the road winding and
meandering along my way only to find
that when I arrive here too is ruined land.

AN ANSWER

Are you happy to return to
civilization? she asked. Happy to
get out of this hellhole happy to
get away? It seemed simple.
I knew what she wanted knew
she wanted me to say Yes knew
I should say Yes in a state filled
with silence.

As I drove home past Dairy
Barn past oil tankers black
like a panther past brick
and stone and wood the radio
played sweet jazz.

IN A LOUNGE IN WILLISTON

Desta sits sidesaddle
on my lap swirls her
drink like a mother
gently stirring soup.
Her shapely legs wrapped
in black tights—a tear
uncovers milk skin as she
shifts her weight to fit my
form. Her wine-laced
voice tingles in my ear
as she whispers,
Take me away from here.

REVELATION

Pastor told me that flares
haunt his dreams.

Grass, he said, grass had gone
missing. Ocean of turf
tossed in the wind.

He said he went blind like Saul, said
he couldn't see anymore, flames
broiled at the back of his neck, sweat
streamed down his back.

He prayed for rain, thought it could
kill the flame like two moist fingers
pinching a candle wick.

But flames grew. Each day he drove
his car the lake of fire grew and he
said he could find no raft.

What would come of it, he asked,
Where would we turn?

Smoldering, he opened the door
to check on the coals in the grill
and the door seemed to flicker.

GOSPEL

In the beginning was the dust
and the dust crumbled
and built a foundation
where the bone cracked
and flesh broke
and leaves fell
where humus built
and oceans foamed
and the dry land bloomed
roses in midnight glow
orbs on the prairie

In the middle time water
and streams flowed
shined copper coins
glinting in the sun cottonwoods
steadied to mark the passage
of water from source to mouth
to belly to body to wash us
in the living thing.

In the end time pump jacks
rose on dry land
black snakes slithered
the horizon a bright orange flame
sent ripples of fear when—
bang—the last bird fell.

DO YOU REMEMBER WHERE YOU LEFT ME

across the gullies of longing, towards
Painted Canyon, where you told me wind
whispers childhood secrets? We sat in sage,
twirled the grey green plant between thumb
and pointer finger, crushed it, like a mortar
and pestle, only to have its scent wrap around our
skin. And what happened to you as we peered
into coal veins, that deep place where diamonds
form, where sun glistens in the flecks of long-
dead plants. Where was your heart at that
moment we climbed over buttes and bluffs
to see bison lumber towards the horizon,
sharp-tailed grouse puff like a red hot balloon in
their fit of lust. Your shoulders sank, as if snow
slid along your ridges, when I told you that
pronghorn no longer call this home, their
palette of brown, white, and black never to
return, you stayed silent like a flickering flame.

KILLDEER MOUNTAIN

A tattered American flag flaps in afternoon
sun, faded, as dry corn stalks crackle beyond
the Killdeer Battlefield. Here, General Sully
ambushed the Lakota, Dakota, and Nakota.
Children screamed, mothers fell like cut
cottonwood trees. Cannons, sent by Lincoln,
hurled lead into the quiet tipis. Indians slipped
past elms, over the tabletop butte, Killdeer
Mountain, to Medicine Hole, oasis of
bleeding people.

III.

JOY

Pick juneberries on ridges of earthen valleys pickle
tomatoes into jars where the smell of sage stings
nostrils, where oceans of clover shock senses like
an electric current jolting a kite. Where the heart feels
the reel of fishing line going downstream like a trout
in a flurry. Good does outweigh bad, refashioning
of tamaracks in golden splendor turn greed green
with envy to dream in the bleak black darkness
of a shifting planet. Plant cottonwoods along river
bottoms, believing tomorrow—somewhere—roots will
hold the world in place.

COMFORT

Cirrus clouds streak cobalt sky
as the sun heats my back, dirt
dusts my shoes, coats my throat
as I drink cool water in rough land.
To hell with convenience, I want
to struggle—to trample through
blonde stubbled fields, the yip
of a prairie dog to my march
up sage-colored switchbacks.
I want my calves to burn,
my muscles to ache
as I navigate prickly pear
and sawgrass. Too many
gadgets in the world—
too much New and Improved.
I want rock, layered by fire,
cut by ice, rippled with water,
to cut my feet, to root me,
to return me to my animal self.

NIGHT AND DAY

I go to bed when birds rise, singing
their sweet and sonorous strains
across the dew wet grass. I go to
bed when the grey blue morning
light filters through my pane like
the slow drip of the morning brew
not yet made. In the midnight of
my fits and flashes I comb the
beach of my mind like a sojourner
looking for a message in a bottle.

Other days I rise when the world
has not yet rubbed its eyes
cleaning sleep from its baby blues
or shook its head to rattle
the imagination of the day. I turn
on a light, a watch-lamp
in the neighborhood, a lighthouse
keeping an eye on sailors. Over the
din of the brewing coffee, I carve
at words like a sculptor with chisels
break away rock reveal the jewel.

LITTLE MISSOURI

Near the Elkhorn Ranch
that cradle of conservation
I stumble past cottonwoods,
grasshoppers, a sea of sage
swept across shallow
river bottom. A lonely place,
for sure, perfect to mend
wounds from a wife lost
in labor, a dead mother.
The noonday sun stings
my back. One eye ahead,
watching for slinking fur,
one eye scanning the ground
for the shake and slide
of scales. Buttes stippled
with switchgrass slide by.
I proceed this way, one
careful step at a time.

SCORIA

In the cracks of your pinkness,
hid from the waiting world
rain and wind beat their way
into your trammeled pathways—
lightning lit the prairie
an electric grid of fire and smoke.

You were meant to be burnt—
to glow through the years,
change and morph, to shed
your skin like a chrysalis
revealing inner beauty.

THEODORE

Perhaps Bully is best before supper
instead of saying grace. To look around
glaring, the world like a mirror struck
with a flashlight, soaking in the lemon-stained
lace across the mahogany table. But Bully
implies a pound, a fistful of fury, it means
to put on your boots, caked with earth
so black it looks like the night sky, to grab
life by its scruffy throat, jingle it like a pocketful
of coins, and clasp your friend's hand one last time.
Did you say it when you slugged Kermit on the
shoulder, when you told him to leave you
in your fevered panic along the Rio da Duvida.
Did you grab that pulpit and smash it against stone
like a porcelain teacup only to holler, *Bring me more.*

AMERICA

To the Captains of Industry,

For selling out for the quick profit,
convenience, and short-term gain,
a royal Fuck You. May you be
skinned alive and set upon
rough-barked scaffold so the hawks
and brown-toned mice may nibble
at your greenback carcasses.

To the Government Officials,

Because, of course you're all *men*,
I'd like to kick you in the balls.
Pride wrapped you in wintertime
as pump jacks pulled dinosaur blood
from deep underground. Hope your testes
hurt as bad as I feel when I look over
broken bentonite bluffs while America
chugs on its way to the fiery sky.

To the Native Americans,

I learned your sacred sites by different
names. Learned that my ancestors *settled*—
or so we thought—the prairie, forced
Sitting Bull to hand over his rifle, the way
of life forever changed, altered, broken.
I don't know the names of sacredness,
only the wind and the word *loneliness*.

To the Future Generations,

I knew better, and so did everyone else. We ate greasy
potato chips, watched reality television while
extinction, desecration, slipped in, while vampires
and werewolves filled the pages, we clapped
with glee. While responsibility skid into complicity,
we turned the volume louder heard the football
score, BMWs rumbled along broken pavement, gazed
at gaudy boob jobs and blow-jobs about to happen.

MEMORY

Enveloped in a sea of golden husks. Stiff and strong,
they prick my face as I lie down. Sun shines, a few
clouds dapple the sky. Wind streaks through golden
waves of grain. This is my America: quiet to most,
insanely alive. My bare legs are the first to rest, then
my bottom, lower and upper back, and finally my head,
upon the coarse soil. Clumps of dirt give way to my
weight and become dust. How unique this is. I never
see anyone else run and disappear in an ocean of wheat.
From afar this looks huge: acres of wheat bursting
through the soil, reaching towards sky, vast and
intimidating. Lying down I am a jungle cat, unseen
and able to surprise anything that comes my way. But
I'm the one who is surprised. Below me are worms,
above me dragonflies hover and hawks look for any field
mouse who leaves the safety of his burrow. I tend to
think this field is chaos, but from down here it's ordered.
And this field is ordered: rows upon rows sewn into the
broken earth, hoped by the farmer that his measly seeds
will break through the earth yet again. I'm thankful for
something as ordinary as this field: it takes me out
of the busyness of my parents' lives and delivers me
into the business of the bees and worms and grain.

WILDNESS RETURN

I.

return to the place
place of longing
longing for the hope
hope of days
days marked by dirt
dirt of familial blood
blood too bitter
bitter dashed dreams
dreams childish things
things caught in the net
net soon lost like a jewel
jewel lost souls wandered
wandered field of clover
clover of kin
kin witness to the ages.

II.

water and wind and soil
rivulets of memory
the prints of my fingertips
soothed the cracks in my skin.

III.

skin brought me back
back to land confused
confused land of greed
greed grew in earth
earth watered by rain
rain across the prairie

prairie of Dakota hearts
hearts pull and pump
pump across time
time too short
short profit of pump jacks.

IV.

prairie of childhood wonder
wandering in time
nestle against broken bark
calms my crackling mind.

V.

mind in love with land
land of mica and quartz
quartz glistens in fossils
fossils rooted to sage
sage fades from the prairie
prairie of stubbled horizon
horizon mixed canyons
canyons scented with clover
clover what I want
want in parched land
land where I miss grass
grass where color
color of sienna brown
brown too drab
drab for the fast
fast-moving world.

VI.

whorled into wildness
land of longing
strut with grouse
rubble from the Rockies
this place knows love.

DELIGHT

I like people who hurl
themselves at their passions
who live inside their furies
who rant and rave. People
who take the months of winter
to build canoes for summer
who knead bread because they
need to smell yeast and flour
dancing to become one.

In my youth I looked, brush in hand,
at the whipping wheat on the berm
behind my house, wondered
What does the bison think?

I fought like a pike with a hook in its mouth,
unrelenting and fierce for a world filled
with the necessity of beauty.
I genuflected to the cottonwoods,
milkvetch, mica-speckled stones
as my chest swelled like the robin's.

CAMELS HUMP BUTTE

too close to Interstate 94
the sound of traffic
drowns the symphony
of meadowlark
horse fly and grasshopper

the summit craggy
strewn with lichen-covered
boulders—green, mustard, seaweed,
burnt orange—faded by the sun

to the east are the Badlands
world worked on slow time
by artisans of water and wind

three black and yellow butterflies
spiral like a trail of smoke higher
and higher, black angus graze
below the base of the butte

wind ripples my cranberry shirt
the sun heats my sweat-soaked neck
I drink cool water from my canteen

up here the dome of the sky immense
clean aquamarine deepening into cobalt

sage and coarse prairie grass—
pretty, sentinel, and bullion buttes
stand silent to the south

rocks upon the ridge bleached bone white—
broken, like a pelvis, from the sand, ice, and wind

mule deer spring across the ridge,
red-winged blackbirds stand watch
the silent butte bears witness

STRUGGLE

On the steppe,
silver sage swings
against a backdrop
of brown earth,
foams near the horizon—
my mind flares with fury.

When blue grama blooms
across the dry lands
stalks unfurl toward sky
buds snap like firecrackers
stiff and golden combing
through the breeze.

Its body sways, three-four time
oom-paa-paa, oom-paa-paa
the flow and pulse across
a floor of dust.

SHOWERING

I didn't shower today
because I felt that damn
good—like a child
swimming in a sandbox
whose hair is filled with
the soil of imagination.
Should I have stayed
in bed, splayed like
a mighty river whose
current is dark and deep?
Where would I have gone?
To church, that hollow
tomb of promises that
leaves me a sojourner in
the night? Maybe to the
store, probing the
archipelagos of my desire,
too deep for friends to
understand. Instead,
I wrote. I cut paper
with pen, pierced
into my caverns
crooked and bright,
like a path illuminated by
fire. The meadowlark
called to me from my
room, like a lover
whispering, Tell me
your wild song.

RADICAL

means to form at the
root, that sturdy place of
support where streams of
water flow upward to aid
the fibrous spread of life.

We will not protect a
place we do not love—
we won't speak for the
speechless.

Friends invite me to their
faraway homes. Elders
tell me: travel when you
are young. See the world
in all its splendor. I
decline my friends but
heed my elders.

I look at the roots of
things—streams,
meadows, oceans,
forests, fungus. I praise
the uniqueness of
sycamores, the necessity
of Norwegian maples.

I may not see the Taj
Mahal, pyramids, or
Machu Picchu, but when
I die let worms weave in
me patterns of passages,
paths trodden and

followed, my hope
to return home to the
root of all I have loved.

I SUPPOSE THE WORLD

                         finds the prairie drab.
Brown, mottled, void of verticality, no
beauty. Blue grama, with its firecracker
head, sways in the sun, and prairie dogs
bark at my strange steps on dry dirt,
genuflect to the cottonwood, sing with
the warble of the yellow-bellied
meadowlark, root myself
like silver sage to a land
that thrums.

BADLANDS

Spine of my childhood
crevices of awe, I clambered
rough bluffs and buttes.
Buoyed by rock and dirt
grass and sage patchwork
of colors on a palette of stone.
Orange, pink, purple, lavender, scarlet
smeared and stippled down sides
of granite and scoria.

Ripped like an abscessed tooth
from a jaw. This land, raw and real,
pushed and pressed to give up
sacred blood: oil. Blood of the land.
My blood. No separation.
Forgiveness from the children
of children yet to come. Plunged
and pulled through pipelines.

Pretty Butte. Bullion Butte. White Butte.
Silent sentinels that mark the passage
of time before we arrived
weather the storm. I sit on soil
and rock. Skin. My skin.
Broken. Bruised. Rippled with the wind,
these ties that bind—dirt, wind, water—
will they wither like a twine cord.

Flares flash in my heart. The horizon
scorches a scene of remorse. The wind
whispers something I cannot hear
and my lungs flare with a desire
for more air. Breath. Life.

Breezes wash my skin as clouds
gather. The horizon bends
like a taut bow, building
with forms shiftless and subtle.

RIVER

I pool
whirl
roil, flow, lift
silt slides like
dark molasses.
Press and rail
against the known
and the new,
burst through barriers,
and break in oxbows.
Am I lazy. Am I flowing
through the motions of
riverbed—squeezing
through crevices
of rock, sand, and sludge.

My current swirls inside
your gullies, pulls you
in the undertow.
Do you quiver
when I touch your skin?
Gush as I wet your hair?
Everything you have built
I will break.

THE CYCLE

And where were you when the
first leaf fell as it flopped
floated its descent to a field
shifted to gold? I watched you
quiver as the first fall chill
cut across your skin.

Winter folded its cold grip
the slashed red of dogwoods gave
hope that grace stumbles—
a prayer crossing a frozen creek.

When tulips pressed and pushed
in the garden you got on your
knees to coat coal black soil
around your flowered vision.

In the light of long days the web
of things—loons whimpering
in twilight frogs in their gurgling
chorus the stars hitched
to the dust of your body.

WAKING UP TO THE WORLD

I turn off my phone so that I can
hear the newspaper whack
the front door. Texts and You've got
mails silenced. The dings pings tings
I look for the pulse that vibrates
to the beat of a world being
made new. Slowing down
it is not easy. The dust of words
settling upon the page, taking pen
in hand to put ink in the book.
Soon the bumble of cars
and the changing lights—
I open the gate and greet the day.

RESISTANCE

Resistance lies in rhythm—
the beat of a heart against
the caverns of our bodies
pump and pull
press and push
the blood ways that pulse
and course through bodies—
and swirls with struggle.

As a child, in swift streams,
water pressed against my
narrow back sent me
downstream. As I skirted along the
stone-lined bottom my
mind flowed into the Missouri
River, past Lake Oahe, along
Iowa, near Nebraska where the
Platte slides in sideways,
pooling, whirling into
the Big Muddy.

My mind flowed on to the
River of Twain's before
emptying into the Gulf
and on into the ocean,
the ripple of our heart.

Where I first learned rhythm
in the body of pole, heaved
fish to shore, the skid of strong
legs, the pull of oar.

Perhaps we know the force
of nature as our bodies
flow inside themselves—resist
the ruin of every living thing.

CREDO
—For David James Duncan

In the beginning God whispered the world into being and the
bluegills I love came into being and the meadowlarks I love
rattled their throats across the sage-scented prairie because a song,
desperate to come out, was inside their wind-whipped bodies, and
the bison wallowed in that gray-colored mud and the sage grouse
did the sagebrush step to the tune of the coyote call rolling across
buttes, bumping over bluffs, snaking through the brown rivers of
the dry heart of the continent, nestled in the nooks and crannies,
and held like a lump of lignite ready to ignite, ready to burn, to
change into the scoria pebbling the roadways, streaking the brown
palette of the prairie in that luscious red smeared on lips that make
clergy simmer in envy because a friend told me that God might
be the Great Mother that adores soft voices, the voices that slip
in sideways, shifting muddy river channels, whorling wood into
mighty river teeth, rolling a single grain of sand one mile every
million years over the bottom down dank mud, through the muck
of a fast-moving world, the open places where ancient sea beds run
through switchgrass where our own soft voice weaves a new song,
and we listen just because it feels that damn good.

ACKNOWLEDGMENTS

Collections do not appear out of thin air and, as a result, words of thanks need to be showered upon the following:

Peter Grimes, Nancy Caine, Herman the Dog and Bailey the Cat, for opening their home to me in western North Dakota during the summer of 2014. Many of these poems were drafted in their home and inspired by the region I call home.

Steve Semken and the Ice Cube Press for saying yes to me, opening the door not only to a rich literary partnership, but a deep and abiding friendship.

Donna Prizgintas, whose sharp wit, keen culinary skill, and constant encouragement is undeserved and much appreciated.

David James Duncan, who has helped open the floodgates of a new way of perceiving the world.

Chip Blake, what is there to say? Thank you for saying Yes to me, and for being my friend.

Scott Gast, brother, with all the baggage it entails.

The Creative Writing and Environment program at Iowa State University, whose gift of time, money, and resources allowed me to develop and grow into the writer I am trying to be.

Patrick Thomas, whose gift of friendship is a needed tonic in my life, and who has opened doors I never dreamed existed.

The Black Earth Institute, and Michael McDermott in particular, whose gift of conversation, resources, and encouragement mean the world to this writer.

Todd and Noah Davis, whose work inspires mine, and whose friendship is bedrock. Tight line!

Karen Wee, whose eye, early on took poems from good to better.

Brenna Gerhardt and the North Dakota Humanities Council: You are a gift to the northern Great Plains. With thanks for bringing me back home time and again.

Frederick Kirschenmann, Carolyn Raffensperger, Jan and Cornelia Flora, for your constant support and help in encouraging the long-view in my own thinking.

To my English teachers: Kathy Lord-Olson, Jane Pole, Jennifer Montgomery, and Jonathan Hill, may this work reflect kindly on you. I will always be your student.

Debra Marquart—friend, teacher, and mentor—from one North Dakotan to another: You are a gift to the wild place we share as home.

Pam Houston, Joe Wilkins, Sean Prentiss, Tyler Dunning, Aimee Nezhukumatathil, Diana Owens, Karen Babine, Alison Deming, Kathleen Dean Moore, Stephen Trimble, Rachel Morgan, Shane Bauer, Anders and Kai Carlson-Wee, David Orr, Kaethe Schwehn, Jeff Lockwood, and Linda Hogan, for the rich literary friendship you've given me.

Diane LeBlanc, whose keen eye saw some potential in a budding poet.

Caroline Nitz, whom I've been trying to live up to since undergraduate, thank you for your support and love.

Abby Travis and Joanna Demkiewicz, sisters to the end.

Andrew Kingsriter and Thomas Christian, Boys and Oil, and brothers in the struggle.

In friendship, Kirsten Brown, John Christian, Bruce Benson, Jon Laven, Mark Odden, Ty Robinson, D.J. Erickson, Kristine Carlson, Morris Wee, Robert and Jane Buckley-Farlee, Maclaine Sorden, Tayo Basquiat, Tom Lamppa, Barb Farrell, Phil and Barb Eaves, Brenda and Richard Jorgenson, Carolyn and Rory Philstrom, Jonathan Steinwand, Amy Weldon, Jon Jensen, John Jensen and Gayle Burdick.

Mary Swander, advocate, friend, and mentor, with thanks for your constant support and the gift of you.

Tanya, Mike, Logan, Noah, Alexander, and Oliver: Without you, I'd have no reason to write.

The following poems appeared, or are forthcoming, in print as earlier versions in the following journals: "Struggle" forthcoming, *ISLE*); "Pallid Sturgeon," (*Canary*, Summer 2015); "The Ages Have Been at Work" (*Bearings*, Spring 2015); "Scoria" and "Delight" (*Written River: Journal of Eco-Poetics* 5.2); "Climbing Buttes" (*The Other Journal* 24, 2015); "The Cycle" (*LETTERS* 3, 2015); "Joy" (*Christmas, Volume Three: He Lays His Glory By*, 2015); "Night and Day" and "Showering" (*About Place Journal: Voices of the Human Spirit 3.2*, 2014); "Prairie" and "Radical"(*EcoTheo Review*, 2014).

Many poems also appeared as earlier versions in my chapbook, *Ruin: Elegies from the Bakken* (2015), through Red Bird Chapbooks; I especially wish to thank Nancy Yoder-Bidwell, whose keen editorial eye made the chapbook better.

Taylor Brorby is an award-winning essayist, and a poet. A fellow at the Black Earth Institute, Taylor's work has appeared in numerous journals and magazines, including *Orion, High Country News, The Huffington Post,* and *Hawk & Handsaw,* and has received numerous recognition through grants and artist residencies. He was recently awarded the new Emerging Critics Fellowship from the National Book Critics Circle.

Taylor travels around the country regularly to speak about hydraulic fracking, is a co-editor of the country's first anthology of creative writing about fracking, *Fracture: Essays, Poems, and Stories on Fracking in America,* and is Reviews Editor at *Orion Magazine.*

The Ice Cube Press began publishing in 1993 to focus on how to live with the natural world. We've since become devoted to using the literary arts to better understand how people can best live together in the communities they share, inhabit, and experience here in the Heartland of the USA. We have been recognized by a number of well-known writers including: Gary Snyder, Gene Logsdon, Wes Jackson, Patricia Hampl, Greg Brown, Jim Harrison, Annie Dillard, Ken Burns, Roz Chast, Jane Hamilton, Daniel Menaker, Kathleen Norris, Janisse Ray, Robert Hass, Alison Deming, Frank Deford, Paul Hawken, Harriet Lerner, Richard Rhodes, Michael Pollan, David Abram, David Orr, Boria Sax, and Barry Lopez. We've published a number of well-known authors including: Governor Robert Ray, Congressman James Leach, Mary Swander, Jim Heynen, Mary Pipher, Bill Holm, Connie Mutel, John T. Price, Carol Bly, Marvin Bell, Debra Marquart, Ted Kooser, Stephanie Mills, Bill McKibben, Craig Lesley, Elizabeth McCracken, Dean Bakopoulos, Dan Gable, Rick Bass, Pam Houston, and Paul Gruchow. Check out Ice Cube Press books on our web site, join our facebook group, follow us on twitter, visit booksellers, museum shops, or any place you can find good books and discover why we continue striving to, "hear the other side."

Ice Cube Press, LLC (Est. 1993)
North Liberty, Iowa 52317-9302
steve@icecubepress.com
twitter: @icecubepress
www.facebook.com/IceCubePress
www.IceCubePress.com

to Fenna Marie
I embrace all your
wishes, hopes & dreams.
You are my greatest creation,
I love you!